'CONTEMPT OF COURT' SUPREME COURT'S LATEST LEADING CASE LAWS

CASE NOTES- FACTS- FINDINGS OF APEX COURT JUDGES & CITATIONS

JAYPRAKASH BANSILAL SOMANI

Copyright © Jayprakash Bansilal Somani
All Rights Reserved.

ISBN 978-1-68487-273-2

This book has been published with all efforts taken to make the material error-free after the consent of the author. However, the author and the publisher do not assume and hereby disclaim any liability to any party for any loss, damage, or disruption caused by errors or omissions, whether such errors or omissions result from negligence, accident, or any other cause.

While every effort has been made to avoid any mistake or omission, this publication is being sold on the condition and understanding that neither the author nor the publishers or printers would be liable in any manner to any person by reason of any mistake or omission in this publication or for any action taken or omitted to be taken or advice rendered or accepted on the basis of this work. For any defect in printing or binding the publishers will be liable only to replace the defective copy by another copy of this work then available.

Dedicated

To

All the Past & Present Judges of the Supreme Court of India.

Salute to their wisdom.

Salute to their interpretation of Law.

Salute to their elaborative judgement writing.

Contents

Preface vii

Acknowledgements ix

1. Committee Of Creditors Of Amtek Auto Limited Through Corporation Bank Vs. Dinkar T. Venkatasubramanian And Ors., 2021 — 1
2. Rama Narang Vs. Ramesh Narang And Ors., 2021 — 4
3. Ashok Kumar And Ors. Vs. The State Of Jammu And Kashmir And Ors., 2021 — 7
4. Madhavi Vs. Chagan And Ors., 2020 — 10
5. In Re: Prashant Bhushan And Ors., 2020 — 12
6. In Re: Vijay Kurle And Ors., 2020 — 15
7. District Bar Association, Dehradun Vs. Ishwar Shandilya And Ors., 2020 — 20
8. Vinay Prakash Singh Vs. Sameer Gehlaut And Ors., 2019 — 23
9. Yashwant Sinha And Ors. Vs. Central Bureau Of Investigation And Ors., 2019 — 25
10. Girish Mittal Vs. Parvati V. Sundaram And Ors., 2019 — 31
11. K. Ananda Rao And Ors. Vs. S. S. Rawat And Ors., 2019 — 34
12. Reliance Communication Limited And Ors. Vs. State Bank Of India And Ors., 2019 — 38
13. Badri Vishal Pandey And Ors. Vs. Rajesh Mittal And Ors., 2019 — 41
14. National Campaign Committee For Central Legislation On Construction Labour (ncc-cl) Vs. Union Of India (uoi) And Ors., 2018 — 44
15. Anil Kalra Vs. J. D. Pandey And Ors., 2015 — 47
16. In Re: Mohit Chaudhary, 2017 — 51
17. Rajiv Dawar Vs. High Court Of Delhi, 2017 — 53
18. Satwant Singh Vs. Malkeet Singh, 2017 — 54

Contents

19. Jaghbir Singh And Ors. Vs. P. K. Tripathi And Ors., 2017	56
20. Vitusah Oberoi And Ors. Vs. Court Of Its Own Motion, 2017	58
Videos & Tv Shows On Law & Exim	61
List Of Books	67

Preface

Dear Learned Advocates of the High Courts, Supreme Court, Corporates & Individuals,

I am very delighted to provide you a book on 'Contempt of Court'- Supreme Court of India's Latest Leading Case Laws'.

In this book you will get...

1. Name of the Case i. e. Cause title
2. Relevant Sections discussed in the case
3. Hon'ble Judges/Coram of the case
4. Number of PDF Pages in Original Judgement of the case
5. All available Citations of the case
6. Case Note with appeal allowed/ dismissed or disposed off
7. Facts of the case
8. Hon'ble Apex Court's findings, while dismissing/allowing or disposing the appeal
9. Ratio Decidendi if any.

My special thanks to Manupatra, because of their web portal I can compile this book in well manner. I am also thankful to Notion Press to support me to publish & market this book throughout the Country. Thanks to my Juniors, Advocate Colleagues & Insolvency Professional Colleagues to support me in this venture.

Miss Simran Mehta has helped me a lot to compile this book.

I hope this book will add some value addition in the wealth of your legal knowledge. Your positive feedbacks will boost me to compile/ write further books & negative feedbacks will improve my skills. Kindly send your valuable feedbacks by email.

Thanks with Regards,
Jayprakash B. Somani
Advocate, Supreme Court of India
Email: jaysomani64@gmail.com
Web Site:www.jayprakashsomani.com
Call:8384051134, 9322188701

Acknowledgements

Printed & Published by
Notion Press
No. 8, 3rd Cross Street,
CIT Colony, Mylapore,
Chennai, Tamil Nadu- 600004

Managed by
Jayprakash Somani Advocates & Solicitors
Law Firm for Supreme Court of India
Delhi Office
257 C, Pocket 1, Mayur Vihar Phase 1, Delhi 110091.
Call 8384051134, 9322188701, 8459194576, 01141051516
Supreme Court Chamber
312, 3rd Floor, M. C. Setalvad Block, In front of 'D' Gate, Bhagwan Das Road, Supreme Court of India, New Delhi 110001
Contact: 8459194576, 9811011747
www.jayprakashsomani.com

Books are available online at
1. Notion Press:https://notionpress.com/author/jayprakash_somani
2. Amazon:https://www.amazon.in/s?k=jayprakash+somani
3. Flipkart:https://www.flipkart.com/search?q=Jayprakash%20Somani

CHAPTER ONE

Committee of Creditors of AMTEK Auto Limited through Corporation Bank Vs. Dinkar T. Venkatasubramanian and Ors., 2021

Relevant Sections: Insolvency And Bankruptcy Code, 2016 - Section 30; Insolvency And Bankruptcy Code, 2016 - Section 31

Hon'ble judges: Dr. D.Y. Chandrachud and M.R. Shah, JJ.

No. of pdf pages in Original Judgment: 17

Equivalent Citations: MANU/SC/0110/2021, 2021(2)RCR(Civil)260

Case note:

Insolvency - Contempt Proceedings - Resolution Plans - Obligations not adhered with - Implications - Resolution plan approved by Committee of Creditors (CoC) of Corporate Debtor - R3 alleged of violating performance of obligations - CoC instituted contempt proceedings, sustainability whereof under challenge - Whether contempt Petition instituted by CoC against R3, Deccan Value Investors LP (DVI) for violation of order maintainable?

Facts:

The present matter pertains to issue of violation of resolution plan by failing to perform obligations. In the instant case, application was filed against the Corporate Debtor and R1 was appointed Resolution Professional (RP). Resolution plans were invited and one by Liberty House Group was approved by the Committee of Creditors (CoC). However, due to violation of resolution plan, CoC sought permission to attempt fresh resolution process. This however was rejected. Rejection followed consequent proceedings at various level RP was approved of issuing fresh invites. Pursuant thereto, plan submitted by Deccan Value Investors LP (DVI) was approved by CoC. Thereafter, DVI sought extension of time so as to understand the implication of COVID-19, a Force Majeure Event, and to re-evaluate the feasibility and viability of the Resolution Plan. The request however was declined by Supreme Court. Meanwhile, Resolution Plan by DVI was approved. DVI filed an Appeal which is pending. CoC then filed a Contempt Petition against DVI for failing to fulfilling its obligations and also obstructing in processes.

Hon'ble Apex court held, while dismissing the application:

There can be no mistaking the fact that DVI, despite having submitted a resolution plan which had undergone discussion and revision before the CoC before being approved in the meeting of the CoC, was seeking to renege its applications to fulfill the resolution plan. The plea for being allowed to re-examine the impact of the pandemic and to re-negotiate the terms of the resolution plan makes it abundantly clear that DVI was not willing to fulfill the terms of the obligations which it had agreed. This is evident from the fact also that though DVI was obliged to furnish the second tranche of its performance bank guarantee, it was not ready to do so. The prayer seeking a direction to allow DVI to extend the bank guarantee was artfully worded since the effect would be to restrain the invocation of the bank guarantee.

The extension of time in the course of the judicial process before this Court enures to the benefit of DVI as a resolution applicant whose proposal was considered under the auspices of the directions of the Court. DVI attempted to resile from its obligations and a reading of its application which led to the passing of the order of Court indicates that DVI was not just seeking an extension of time but a re-negotiation of its resolution plan after its approval by the CoC. The conduct of DVI lacked in bona fides. The default of DVI, however, in fulfilling the terms of the resolution plan may invite consequences as envisaged in law. On the balance, it was held as not appropriate to exercise the contempt jurisdiction of this Court.

No merit in the application for rectification and hence dismissed. It is not expedient in the interest of justice to pursue the contempt proceedings and thus the contempt Petition (C) No. 524 of 2020 in Civil Appeal No. 6707 of 2019 dismissed. However, in terms of the submission made by DVI as a consequence of the dismissal of its Interim Application, it shall not set-up a plea for force majeure in the proceedings pending before the NCLAT in appeal against the order of NCLT approving resolution plan.

CHAPTER TWO

Rama Narang Vs. Ramesh Narang and Ors., 2021

Relevant Sections: Companies Act, 1956 - Section 397; Companies Act, 1956 - Section 398; Companies Act, 1956 - Section 403; Contempt Of Courts Act, 1971 - Section 2

Hon'ble judges: A.M. Khanwilkar and B.R. Gavai, JJ.

No. of pdf pages in Original Judgment: 32

Equivalent Citations: AIR2021SC721, MANU/SC/0025/2021

Case note:

Contempt of Court - Consent order - Wilful disobedience - Respondent No. 1 had approached this Court by filing Contempt Petition in Contempt Petition whereby this court satisfied that contemnor had flouted order of this Court by not transferring half of share - Subsequently matter was settled between parties and parties had placed on record Minutes of Consent Order which was family settlement between all members of family including parties herein - This court affirmed said Minutes of Consent Order - Petitioner alleging, that Respondents had violated terms of Consent Order stipulated in Minutes of Consent Order - Hence, present contempt petition - Whether violations of Consent Order by Respondents amounted to clear disobedience of orders passed by this court and punishable under Contempt of Courts Act, 1971.

Facts:

The Respondent No. 1 had approached this Court by filing a Contempt Petition whereby this court satisfied that the contemnor had flouted the order of this Court by not transferring half of the share. Subsequently the matter was settled between the parties and the parties had placed on record the Minutes of the Consent Order which was a family settlement between all the members of the family including the parties herein. Petitioner alleging, that Respondents had violated the terms of the Consent Order stipulated in the Minutes of the Consent Order, filed a contempt petition. It was the case of the Petitioner that the violations of the Consent Order by Respondents amounted to clear disobedience of the orders and thus punishable under the Contempt of Courts Act, 1971.

Hon'ble Apex court held, while dismissing the petition:

(i) In the present case, undisputedly, the Respondents were entitled to invoke the jurisdiction of the CLB under Sections 397, 398 and 403 of the Companies Act. The CLB had passed the order appointing a Facilitator and further passed order enhancing the powers of the Facilitator. Perusal of the orders passed by this Court would reveal, that though this Court had appointed independent Director, it is clarified, that the independent Director's functioning would not come in the way of the functioning of the Facilitator. On the contrary, this Court observed, that the appointment independent Director would facilitate the functioning of the Facilitator, appointed by the CLB.

(ii) The Petitioner had failed to make out a case of wilful, deliberate and intentional disobedience of any of the directions given by this Court or acting in breach of an undertaking given to this Court. On the contrary, we find that the Respondents had taken recourse to the legal remedy available to them under the statutory provisions.

(iii) It was not in dispute, that the order of CLB had not been challenged by the Petitioner before any forum. The observations were indisputably adverse to the case of the Petitioner. Any order passed by the CLB was appealable before the higher forums. Undisputedly, the Petitioner had not challenged the said order. Having not challenged the same, it was not open for the Petitioner to argue, that since the Petitioner had taken objection as to maintainability of the proceedings before CLB, the said orders were without jurisdiction and the initiation of the proceedings and the orders passed thereon, would amount to Respondent's committing contempt of this Court. The argument needs to be rejected, in view of the judgment of this Court in the case of Tayabbhai M. Bagasarwalla. This Court in unequivocal terms has held, that even if the objection is raised to the jurisdiction of a forum, it has jurisdiction to pass interim orders till it finally decides the issue of jurisdiction and such orders are binding on the parties till the issue of jurisdiction is decided. As could be seen from the order of the CLB, though the CLB by referring to Sections 397, 398 and 399 of the Companies Act, prima facie, had observed, that only if maintainability was challenged either in terms of Section 399 of the Companies Act or on the ground of jurisdiction of the Board, the same would have to be considered first and challenges on other grounds, had to be considered along with the merits of the case. The CLB had further observed, that it was an admitted fact, that the Petitioner qualifies under Section 399 of the Act and the Court has the jurisdiction to deal with the petition under Section 397 or/and 398 of the Act. Having chosen not to challenge the said observations of the CLB, the argument advanced deserves no merit and needs to be rejected. However, it should not be construed, that this court had held that the proceedings under the CLB were maintainable in law. Since the proceedings were pending final adjudication, the parties would be at liberty to raise all issues available to them including the issue of jurisdiction.

CHAPTER THREE

Ashok Kumar and Ors. Vs. The State of Jammu and Kashmir and Ors., 2021

Relevant Sections: Constitution Of India - Article 14; Constitution Of India - Article 16

Hon'ble judges:S.A. Bobde, C.J.I., A.S. Bopanna and V. Ramasubramanian, JJ.

No. of pdf pages in Original Judgment: 7

Equivalent Citations:AIR2021SC548, 2021LabIC573, (2021)ILLJ481SC, MANU/SC/0023/2021, 2021(1)SCT363(SC), 2021(1)SLJ408(SC), 2021(2)SLR234(SC)

Case note:

Service - Promotion - Qualifications thereto - Appellants were directly recruited as Junior Assistants with qualification of graduation, were promoted as Head Assistants from post of Senior Assistants - Some vacancies were available and hence contesting Respondents were also promoted as Head Assistants - Challenging the promotions so granted to contesting Respondents, one ground that they were not qualified at relevant point of time, writ petition was filed - Writ petition was allowed and order of promotion of Respondents was set aside - As consequence thereof, all persons like Appellants, who were left out earlier, were promoted as Head Assistants - Finding that benefit promotion that came to them was short lived and also finding that this was on account of office order of Chief Justice, contesting Respondents filed writ petitions - Single Judge, quashed administrative Order of Chief Justice prescribing certain qualifications for promotion to post of Head Assistant along with power of relaxation, persons who were fully qualified as per Rules at time of appointment -

Appellants filed appeals which were dismissed by Division Bench of High Court - Hence, present appeal - Whether High Court erred in quashing administrative Order of Chief Justice prescribing certain qualifications for promotion to post of Head Assistant.

Facts:

The contesting private Respondents were originally appointed as peons (Class-IV). They were promoted as Junior Assistants and as Senior Assistants. The Appellants who were directly recruited as Junior Assistants with the qualification of graduation, were promoted as Head Assistants from the post of Senior Assistants. It appears that still some vacancies were available and hence the contesting Respondents who entered service as Class-IV employees and who had risen upto the position of Senior Assistants, were also promoted as Head Assistants. However, such promotions were intended to fill up the gap till eligible candidates were available. Challenging the promotions so granted to the contesting Respondents-herein, on the ground that they were not qualified at the relevant point of time, a writ petition in Writ Petition was filed. The writ petition was allowed and the Order of the promotion of the contesting Respondents was set aside. The affected parties filed appeals but those appeals were dismissed. As a consequence thereof, all persons like the Appellants-herein, who were left out earlier, were promoted as Head Assistants. Finding that the benefit promotion that came to them was short lived and also finding that this was on account of the office Order of the Chief Justice, the contesting Respondents-herein filed a set of writ petitions. Single Judge, quashed an administrative Order of the Chief Justice prescribing certain qualifications for promotion to the post of Head Assistant along with a power of relaxation, persons who were fully qualified as per the Rules at the time of appointment. Challenging the Order of Single Judge passed in favour of the contesting Respondents, the Appellant filed a set of Letters Patent Appeals. These appeals were dismissed by a Division Bench of the High Court.

Hon'ble Apex court held, while allowing the appeal:

(i) As a matter of fact, the Order of promotion promoting the contesting Respondents as Head Assistants made it clear that their appointments were only till eligible and suitable candidates were posted to these posts and that they could be considered for regularisation/appointment only if they attain the qualification and experience prescribed for the post. But the contesting Respondents did not choose to challenge the Order of Chief Justice, until the writ petition filed against their promotion was allowed by the single Judge and the Order also got confirmed in writ appeal by the Division Bench.

(ii) It was clear that the power of the Chief Justice clearly flowed out of Rule 6 of the Jammu & Kashmir High Court Staff (Conditions of Service) Rules, 1968. These Rules were issued by the High Court in exercise of the power conferred by Section 108(2) of the Constitution of Jammu & Kashmir. These Rules had the approval of the Governor also. Therefore, the contention of the Respondents that the office order issued by the Chief Justice was ultra vires, was completely untenable.

(iii) The High Court was wrong in thinking that Note-2 of the Order of the Chief Justice curtailed or restricted the power of relaxation available with him. If the authority conferred with the power to relax, chooses to regulate the manner of exercise of his own power, the same could not be assailed as arbitrary. The notification prescribed for the first time, graduation as a necessary qualification. This was why, the Chief Justice chose by his Order, to limit his own power of relaxation to cases where appointments were made before the cut off date.

(iv) The contention that the Order of the Chief Justice affects the staff adversely with retrospective effect, was completely incorrect. The Order did not at all impact the promotions gained by persons. The entitlement of unqualified candidates to seek promotion to the post of Head Assistant was what was impacted by the Order of the Chief Justice.

(v) The High Court erred in thinking that the impugned action of the Chief Justice violated Article 14 by creating a distinction between graduates and non graduates among the same category of persons who constituted a homogenous class.

CHAPTER FOUR

Madhavi Vs. Chagan and Ors., 2020

Relevant Sections: Maharashtra Employees Of Private Schools (Conditions Of Service) Regulation Act, 1977 - Section 5(5)

Hon'ble judges:L. Nageswara Rao, Hemant Gupta and Ajay Rastogi, JJ.

No. of pdf pages in Original Judgment: 13

Equivalent Citations:2021(1)BLJ167, 2020(4)LLN529(SC), MANU/SC/0929/2020, 2021 (1) SCJ 173

Case note:

Service - Promotion - Post of 'Head Master' - Seniority - Determination thereof - Section 5(5) of the Maharashtra Employees of Private Schools (Conditions of Service) Regulation Act, 1977 - The Maharashtra Employees of Private Schools (Conditions of Service) Rules, 1981 - Appellant's promotion to post of Head Master challenged - Respondent contended promotion to be illegal as Appellant even employed earlier was not regular - Appellant's seniority was challenged - Whether Appellant was wrongly considered above in seniority over Respondent for promotion?

Facts:

The present dispute was in respect of appointment of Appellant as the Head Master of the School. Respondent claimed that he was appointed on regular basis on 1.8.1985 as against Appellant who was appointed against a temporary vacancy on 16.7.1985. Respondent challenged the appointment contending that he is senior to Appellant and in terms of the Rules, he would be entitled to be promoted as Head Master. School Tribunal dismissed the plea. High Court also dismissed the appeal with the detailed reasoning. An application for review was then filed and the same was allowed vide impugned judgment.

Hon'ble Apex court held, while allowing the appeal:

i. High Court failed to appreciate the distinction between Clause 1 and Clause 2 of Schedule 'F' of the Rules. Clause 1 was the subject matter of interpretation by this Court in VimanVamanAwale and Clause 2 was the subject matter of interpretation in Bhawna. Vaijanath also dealt with promotion to the post of Head Master of a School falling in Clause 1 of Schedule 'F'. Since the School in question is a secondary school, therefore, Clause 2 of Schedule 'F' will determine the seniority. Chagan was not a trained teacher to be part of Category 'C' at the time of his appointment on 1.8.1985 and he was rightly placed in Category 'E' on account of his qualification but he upgraded his qualifications, and hence was placed in Category 'D' and 'C' on acquiring graduation and B.Ed. degrees respectively.

ii. Keeping in view the principle laid down in Vaijanath, Madhavi was qualified for appointment as a temporary teacher as she was a graduate and also possessed B.Ed. degree. Her appointment was thus in accordance with Section 5(5) of the Act, so was the appointment of the other private Respondents. However, Chagan could not be treated to be part of Category 'C' from the date of his initial appointment i.e. 1.8.1985 as he was neither a graduate nor a trained teacher when he was appointed. Also, Chagan was not even a trained teacher on the date of his appointment and thus cannot claim seniority on such ground from the date of his initial appointment.

iii. Thus, the judgment of the High Court in review cannot be sustained in law and the same is hence set aside. The Writ Petition is ordered to be dismissed. The present appeals allowed and the contempt petition also dismissed.

CHAPTER FIVE

In Re: Prashant Bhushan and Ors., 2020

Relevant Sections: Constitution Of India - Article 19(1); Constitution Of India - Article 19(2)

Hon'ble judges: Arun Mishra, B.R. Gavai and Krishna Murari, JJ.

No. of pdf pages in Original Judgment: 42

Equivalent Citations: AIR2020SC4114, 2020 (3) ALT (Crl.) 211 (A.P.), (2020)7MLJ193, MANU/SC/0653/2020, 2020(3)RCR(Criminal)793, (2021)3SCC160

Case note:

Contempt of Court - Contempt proceedings - Suo Moto cognizance - Plea of 'Truth' raised as defence - Whether statements damaging the reputation of judicial institution can be termed as made bonafide in the public interest? - Conviction was directed - Court had to make pronouncement on sentence.

Facts:

After having adjudged Shri Prashant Bhushan, Advocate, guilty of contempt it was argued on sentence that since with respect to first tweet, copy of petition was not furnished, in spite of the application having been filed by the contemnor. Thus, it could not be ascertained whether the complaint was mala fide or even personally or politically motivated. Further, the factors relevant for sentencing are the offender, the offence, the convicting judgment, statutory or other defences relating to a substantial interference with justice, truth, bona fides, and public interest in disclosure. The contemnor is a lawyer of 35 years of standing, who has pursued public interest litigation successfully at some personal and professional cost and has got appreciation from the Court. On contempt there are various guidelines laid down by the Court. They are, free market of ideas, fair criticism in good faith when it is in the public interest, the surrounding circumstances, the person who is making the comments, his knowledge in the field regarding which the comments are made and the intended purpose. After considering all these guidelines, an advocate should be punished by exercising extreme caution only in the case where the tendency is to create disaffection and disrepute to erode the judicial system. Though the convicting judgment, on the one hand cites various decision on balance, on the contrary holds the contemnor guilty for the fair criticism made by him. Besides that, provisions in Sections 8 and 9 and newly amended Section 13(a) of the Act requires that the Court cannot impose a sentence unless it is satisfied that contempt is of such a nature that substantially interferes or tends substantially to interfere with the due course of justice. Thus, special responsibility is cast on the Court to examine the extent of interference. The provisions of newly amended Section 13(a) amply make it clear that the Court is required to assess the situation itself. With respect to the second tweet, this was again an expression of opinion by Shri Prashant Bhushan. The defence of truth was not examined at all in the convicting judgment and the same needs to be examined at the stage of sentencing in compliance with Section 13(b) of the Act. Freedom of speech cannot be snatched of anyone.

Hon'ble Apex court held, while disposing the matter:

The defence taken in the affidavit cannot be said to be either bona fide or in the public interest. Both the tweets coupled with averments in the reply affidavit are capable of shaking the confidence of the public in the institution as a whole. The second tweet is capable of creating an impression that the entire Supreme Court in the last six years has played a vital role in the destruction of democracy.

It is not expected of a person who is a part of the system of administration of justice and who owes a duty to the said system, to make such tweets which are capable of shaking the confidence of general public and further making wild allegations in the affidavit thereby further attempting to malign the said institution. Such an act by responsible person who is part of this system cannot be ignored or overlooked.

There is no justification to make such a remark/tweet, particularly when it is made by a lawyer with 35 years standing like Shri Prashant Bhushan, who is an officer of the Court and advocates enjoy equal dignity in the system.

The Court, from the very beginning, was desirous of giving quietus to this matter. Directly or indirectly, the contemnor was persuaded to end this matter by tendering an apology and save the grace of the institution as well as the individual, who is an officer of the Court. However, for the reasons best known to him he has neither shown regret in spite of our persuasion or the advice of the learned Attorney General.

The act committed by the contemnor is a very serious one. He has attempted to denigrate the reputation of the institution of administration of justice of which he himself is a part. At the cost of repetition, we have to state that the faith of the citizens of the country in the institution of justice is the foundation for Rule of law which is an essential factor in the democratic set up.

The contemnor not only gave wide publicity to the second statement submitted before this Court on 24.08.2020 prior to the same being tendered to the Court, but also gave various interviews with regard to sub judice matter, thereby further attempting to bring down the reputation of this Court.

The contemnor punished with a fine or Re. 1/- (Rupee one) to be deposited with the Registry by date specified, failing which to undergo a simple imprisonment for a period of three months and further be debarred from practising in this Court for a period of three years.

CHAPTER SIX

In Re: Vijay Kurle and Ors., 2020

Relevant Sections: Constitution Of India - Article 129; Constitution Of India - Article 142

Hon'ble judges: Deepak Gupta and Aniruddha Bose, JJ.

No. of pdf pages in Original Judgment: 38

Equivalent Citations: AIR2020SC3927, 2021(1)ALD65, 2020(3)MLJ(Crl)421, MANU/SC/0413/2020, 2020 (5) SCJ 1

Case note:

Contempt of Court - Scandalous allegations - Guilty of - Section 15 of Contempt of Courts Act, 1971 - Letter was sent by Contemnors to President of India, Chief Justice of India and Chief Justice of Bombay High Court - Complaints attached to said letter made scandalous allegations against members of Bench - Hence, present contempt petition - Whether contemnors were guilty of contempt of court by making scandalous allegations against members of Bench.

Facts:

A Bench of this Court while dealing with Suo Motu Contempt Petition took note of a letter received by the office of the Judges of the Bench. This was a copy of the letter sent to the President of India, Chief Justice of India and the Chief Justice of the High Court. In the said letter, reference was made to two complaints one made by the contemnor No. 1 and the second complaint made by alleged contemnor No. 2. It was mentioned that these complaints had not only been sent to the President of India and the Chief Justice of India but also had been circulated in the social media. The Bench took note of the letter and the complaints attached to the said letter and specifically noted the prayers made in both the complaints and found that both the complaints were substantially similar. The Bench on noting the allegations made in the complaints was of the view that scandalous allegations had been made against the members of the said Bench and, therefore, contempt proceedings initiated against contemnors.

Hon'ble Apex court held, while listing the matter:

(i) The powers of the Supreme Court to initiate contempt were not in any manner limited by the provisions of the Act. This Court is vested with the constitutional powers to deal with the contempt. Section 15 is not the source of the power to issue notice for contempt. It only provides the procedure in which such contempt is to be initiated and this procedure provides that there are three ways of initiating a contempt suo motu, on the motion by the Advocate General/Attorney General/Solicitor General and on the basis of a petition filed by any other person with the consent in writing of the Advocate General/Attorney General/Solicitor General. As far as suo motu petitions were concerned, there was no requirement for taking consent of anybody because the Court was exercising its inherent powers to issue notice for contempt. This was not only clear from the provisions of the Act but also clear from the Rules laid down by this Court.

(ii) It was true that the Chief Justice is the master of the roster and in normal course a matter can be listed before a Bench only on the basis of orders issued by the Chief Justice. However, here the situation was totally different. The Bench was already dealing with Suo Motu Contempt Petition. The letter was placed before the Bench. Along with this letter the complaints filed by contemnors were annexed. The Bench took suo motu notice of the allegations made in these two complaints and directed that contempt proceedings be initiated. Thereafter, in accordance with the principles of natural justice and also the principle that the Chief Justice is the master of the roster the Bench directed that the matter may be listed before the Chief Justice for placing it before the appropriate Bench. The Chief Justice, though no doubt, master of the roster, was first amongst the equals and every Judge of the Supreme Court was as much part of this Court as the Chief Justice. The Judges of this Court could exercise their powers under Article 129 of the Constitution which is a constitutional power untrammelled by any Rules or convention to the contrary. Even so, the Bench in deference to the principle of master of the roster, after taking cognizance of the scandalous allegations made in the complaints of the alleged contemnors and issuing notice to them directed that the matter be placed before the Chief Justice for listing before an appropriate Bench. This, was the proper procedure. If an article, letter or any writing or even something visual circulating in electronic, print or social media or in any other forum is brought to the notice of any Judge of this Court which prima facie shows that the allegation is contemptuous or scandalises the court then that Judge can definitely issue notice and thereafter place it before the Chief Justice for listing it before an appropriate Bench.

(iii) The disclosure of the information was made in the order itself where it was clearly recorded that the action had been taken on the basis of the letter sent to the President of India and the Chief Justice of India in response to the complaints made by the alleged contemnors. The complaints of contemnors were also attached with the letters and after taking note not only of the letter but also the prayer clauses of both the complaints sent by the alleged contemnors and the scandalous allegations made in the complaints, the notice was issued. The source of information was the letter sent, as was apparent from the order initiating contempt proceedings.

(iv) Both the complaints were ex-facie contemptuous. Highly scurrilous and scandalous allegations have been levelled against the two judges of this Court. The entire contents of the complaints amount to contempt. Since both the complaints run into more than two hundred fifty pages it was not possible to quote the entire complaints and we are dealing with some of the more scandalous allegations levelled in the said complaints.

(v) The alleged contemnors could had criticised the correctness of the judgment, but the allegation that observations of one judge of Bench amount to contempt of Court or show his poor level of understanding and lack of basic understanding of law was not language which a lawyer is expected to use against a sitting Judge of the Supreme Court. Again, in this very quoted portion a totally unfounded allegation has been made that one judge of bench was aggrieved since allegations had been levelled against his close Judge of the High Court. The conclusion drawn by contemnor no.1 was not only incorrect but totally false and appears to have been done with the mala fide intention of harming the reputation of judge of the bench and raising questions with regard to his impartiality or ability. In fact, Writ Petition was filed by contemnor no.4 before the High Court praying that criminal action under Contempt of Courts Act be initiated against one judge of the High Court. This writ petition was dismissed by the High Court. The High Court did not decide whether contemnor no.4 had committed contempt of Court or not. But the allegations made by contemnor no.4 were not accepted. This means that the High Court did not find any merit in the petition of contemnor no.4 and dismissed the same. Nothing had been placed on record to show that this judgment was under challenge before this Court. The High Court was not dealing with the contempt proceedings. The Bench has only relied upon the judgment to support his observation that contemnor no.4 was in the habit of making such accusations against sitting Judges of the Court.

(vi) No doubt, any citizen can comment or criticise the judgment of this Court. However, that citizen must have some standing or knowledge before challenging the ability, capability, knowledge, honesty, integrity, and impartiality of a Judge of the highest court of the land. The complaint of contemnor no.1 was full of mistakes and he had not even cared to check the spelling of the name of the Judge who he claims had no knowledge of law. His professional credentials were not known and fail to understand how could he adorn the robes of a Judge to pass judgment on the Judges of the highest court, that too by using highly intemperate language and language which casts a doubt not only on the ability of the Judges but scandalises the Court and lowers the dignity and reputation of this Court in the eyes of the general public. These sort of scandalous allegations had to be dealt with sternly and nipped in the bud. As far as contemnor no.2 was concerned, he professes to be the National Secretary of an NGO. Other than that, it did not even appear that he was a lawyer. What was the public interest in raking up issues with regard to a litigation which had no element of public interest. It deals mainly with quashing of the proceedings initiated by the High Court against a party under Section 340 of the Code of Criminal Procedure. There was no explanation as to what the case of Aarish Asgar Qureshi had got to do with this case. It was not as if somebody has been put behind bars or the human rights of any person had been violated. The contemnor no.2 was basically waging a war against the Members of the Bench and against this Court at the instance of contemnor no.3, if not contemnor no.4 because in his complaint he states that contemnor no.3 was the lawyer for the Respondent before the Court and could be the only person who could have supplied the material to contemnor no.2.

(vii) The complaint sent by contemnor no.1 was in connivance and at the behest of contemnor no. 3. Therefore, all three contemnors were working in tandem and making scurrilous and scandalous allegations against the Members of the Bench, probably with the intention that the Members of the Bench would thereafter not take action against contemnor no.4.

CHAPTER SEVEN

District Bar Association, Dehradun Vs. Ishwar Shandilya and Ors., 2020

Relevant Sections: Constitution Of India - Article 14; Constitution Of India - Article 21

   Hon'ble judges: Arun Mishra and M.R. Shah, JJ.

   No. of pdf pages in Original Judgment: 16

   Equivalent Citations: AIR2020SC1412, 2020(8)ADJ159, 2020(2)ALT164, 2020(2)J.L.J.R.45, 2020(4)MPLJ87, 2020(5)MhLJ303, MANU/SC/0235/2020, 2020(2)PLJR45, 2020(2)ShimLC977, 2020 (3) SCJ 189

   Case note:

Constitution - Right to strike - Directions thereto - Advocates in entire District of Dehradun, in several districts of Haridwar and Udham Singh Nagar district in State of Uttarakhand had been boycotting Courts on all Saturdays for past more than thirty five years - As strikes were seriously obstructing access to justice to needy litigants, Respondent No. 1 was compelled to approach High Court - High Court was of opinion that on all such working days on account of strikes and the conduct of Advocates in boycotting Courts, it had affected functioning of Courts and it contributes to ever-mounting pendency of cases, and therefore certain directions had been issued by High Court - Hence, present appeal - Whether directions issued by High Court to District Bar Associations of State of Dehradun to withdraw their call for strike, and start attending Courts on all working Saturdays warrant any interference.

   Facts:

The advocates in the entire District of Dehradun, in several districts of Haridwar and Udham Singh Nagar district in the State of Uttarakhand had been boycotting the Courts on all Saturdays for the past more than thirty years. As the strikes are seriously obstructing the access to justice to the needy litigants, Respondent No. 1 was compelled to approach the High Court by way of Writ Petition (PIL). Having noted from the information sent by the High Court to the Law Commission that with respect to the State of Uttarakhand, the High Court was of the opinion that on all such working days on account of strikes and the conduct of the Advocates in boycotting Courts, it had affected the functioning of the Courts and it contributes to the ever-mounting pendency of the cases, and therefore directions had been issued by the High Court. The High Court directed District Bar Associations of Dehradun, Haridwar and Udham Singh Nagar shall, forthwith, withdraw their call for a strike, and start attending Courts on all working Saturdays. All the District Bar Associations in the State shall forthwith refrain from abstaining from Courts because of condolence references for family members of Advocates, or for other reasons. In case they did not start attending Courts, as directed hereinabove, the District Judges concerned shall submit their respective reports to the High Court for it to consider whether action should be initiated against the errant Advocates under the Contempt of Courts Act.

Hon'ble Apex court held, while dismissing the appeal:

(i) This Court time and again deprecated the lawyers to go on strikes, the strikes were continued unabated. Even in the present case, the advocates had been boycotting the courts on all Saturdays, in the entire district of Dehradun, in several parts of the district of Haridwar and Udham Singh Nagar district of the State of Uttaranchal. Because of such strikes, the ultimate sufferers were the litigants. From the data mentioned in the impugned judgment and order, things were very shocking. Every month on third-fourth Saturdays, the Advocates were on strike and abstain from working, on one pretext or the other. If the lawyers would have worked on those days, it would have been in the larger interest and it would have achieved the ultimate goal of speedy justice, which was now recognized as a fundamental right under Articles 14 and 21 of the Constitution. It would have helped in early disposal of the criminal trials and therefore it would have been in the interest of those who were languishing in the jail and waiting for their trial to conclude. When the Institution was facing a serious problem of arrears and delay in disposal of cases, how the Institution as a whole could afford such four days strike in a month.

(ii) So far as the submission on behalf of the Petitioner that to go on strike/boycott courts was a fundamental right of Freedom of Speech and Expression under Article 19(1)(a) of the Constitution and it was a mode of peaceful representation to express the grievances by the lawyers' community was concerned, such a right to freedom of speech could not be exercised at the cost of the litigants and/or at the cost of the Justice Delivery System as a whole. To go on strike/boycott courts could not be justified under the guise of the right to freedom of speech and expression under Article 19(1)(a) of the Constitution. Nobody had the right to go on strike/boycott courts. Even, such a right, if any, could not affect the rights of others and more particularly, the right of Speedy Justice guaranteed under Articles 14 and 21 of the Constitution. In any case, all the said submissions were already considered by this Court earlier and more particularly in the decisions referred. Therefore, boycotting courts on every Saturday in the entire District of Dehradun, in several districts of Haridwar and Udham Singh Nagar district in the State of Uttarakhand was not justifiable at all and as such it tantamounts to contempt of the courts, as observed by this Court in the said decisions. Therefore, the High Court was absolutely justified in issuing the impugned directions. This court was in complete agreement with the view expressed by the High Court and the ultimate conclusion and the directions issued by the High Court.

Ratio Decidendi:

To go on strike/boycott courts cannot be justified under the guise of the right to freedom of speech and expression under Article 19(1)(a) of the Constitution.

CHAPTER EIGHT

Vinay Prakash Singh Vs. Sameer Gehlaut and Ors., 2019

Relevant Sections: Contempt Of Courts Act, 1971 - Section 2(b)

   Hon'ble judges: Ranjan Gogoi, C.J.I., Deepak Gupta and Sanjiv Khanna, JJ.

   No. of pdf pages in Original Judgment: 16

   Equivalent Citations:(2019)8MLJ498, MANU/SC/1582/2019, 2019(16)SCALE527

   Case note:

Contempt of Court - Disobedience of order - Dispute between Petitioner and Respondents was referred to international arbitration in which arbitral award was passed - Petitioner filed proceedings for enforcement of foreign award in High Court - Respondents filed objections which were dismissed - Challenge to judgment of High Court had been rejected by this Court - This Court directed that status quo with regard to shareholding of company shall be maintained.- It was alleged that transfer of shares was in contempt of orders passed by this Court - Hence, present petition - Whether contemnors No.1-8 were guilty of knowingly and wilfully disobeying the orders of this Court.

   Facts:

A dispute between the Petitioner and the Respondents was referred to international arbitration. An arbitral award was passed whereby the Petitioner was held entitled to receive certain sum from Respondent No. 1 to 15. The Petitioner filed proceedings for the enforcement of the foreign award in Delhi High Court. The Respondents No. 1 to 15 in the SLP objected to the same and filed objections under Section 48 of the Arbitration and

Conciliation Act, 1996. These objections were dismissed except insofar as Respondents No. 5 and 9 to 12 before the High Court were concerned since these Respondents were minors. The challenge to the judgment of the High Court has been rejected by this Court. This Court directed that status quo with regard to shareholding of company shall be maintained. It was alleged that the transfer of shares was in contempt of orders passed by this Court.

Hon'ble Apex court held, while allowing the appeal:

(i) This Court directed that status quo with regard to shareholding of companies be maintained. It was clarified that the order would apply to both encumbered and unencumbered shares. Unencumbered shares were pledged in favour of company. As far as this violation of the order was concerned, the same stands condoned. This would further mean that the unencumbered shares should have been reduced.

(ii) The company, in fact, flagrantly violated this Court's orders and made various transactions transferring even unencumbered shares. The best course available to company would have been to approach this Court seeking a clarification before it made the transfers. This they did not do. therefore, contemnor Nos. 1 to 8 knowing fully well that this Court had passed an order directing status quo to be maintained with regard to the holding of shares, violated the order. There could be no manner of doubt that contemnors had violated these orders and, therefore, contemnor Nos. 1-8 were guilty of knowingly and wilfully disobeying the orders of this Court and find them guilty of committing Contempt of Court.

CHAPTER NINE

Yashwant Sinha and Ors. Vs. Central Bureau of Investigation and Ors., 2019

Relevant Sections: Prevention Of Corruption Act, 1988 - Section 17-A; Code of Civil Procedure, 1908 (CPC) - Order XLVII Rule 1; Constitution Of India - Article 137

Hon'ble judges: Ranjan Gogoi, C.J.I., Sanjay Kishan Kaul and K.M. Joseph, JJ.

No. of pdf pages in Original Judgment: 36

Equivalent Citations: 2019(4)MLJ(Crl)539, MANU/SC/1564/2019, 2019(16)SCALE1, (2020)2SCC338

Case note:

Criminal -Investigation - Maintainability of review petition- Section 340 of the Code of Criminal Procedure, 1973 (CrPC) Section 17 A of Prevention of Corruption (Amendment) Act, 2018; Article 32 of Constitution of India, 1950 - Common judgment in four Writ Petitions had generated three Review Petitions, a Contempt Petition and a Petition under Section 340 of CrPC and an application seeking correction - Review Petition was filed by Petitioners in Writ Petition, in the said Writ Petition, relief sought, was to register an FIR and to investigate the complaint which was made by Petitioners and to submit periodic status reports - Whether review applications were required to be entertained.

Facts:

Review Petition was filed by Petitioners in Writ Petition. In the said Writ Petition, relief sought, was to register an FIR and to investigate the complaint which was made by Petitioners and to submit periodic status reports. Issue is relating to limited judicial review, available to the Court.

Hon'ble Apex court held, while dismissing review petitions:
Sanjay Kishan Kaul, J.

1. Unless there is an error apparent on the face of the record, these review applications are not required to be entertained.

2. Present Court have dealt with the pleas of the learned Counsel for the parties in order dated 14.12.2018 under the heads of 'Decision Making Process', 'Pricing' and 'Offsets'. However, before proceeding to deal with these aspects, present had set out the contours of the scrutiny in matters of such a nature. The extent of permissible judicial review in matters of contract, procurement, etc. would vary with the subject matter of the contract and that there cannot be a uniform standard of depth of judicial review which could be understood as an across the board principle to apply to all cases of award of work or procurement of goods/material.

3. Present Court is dealing with a contract for aircrafts, which was pending before different Governments for quite some time and the necessity for those aircrafts has never been in dispute.

4. In the course of the review petitions, it was canvassed that reliance had been placed by the Government on patently false documents.

5. The other aspect sought to be raised specifically in Review Petition No. 46/2019 is that the prayer made by the Petitioner was for registration of an F.I.R. and investigation by the C.B.I., which has not been dealt with and the contract has been reviewed prematurely by the Judiciary without the benefit of investigation and inquiry into the disputed questions of facts.

6. Present Court do not consider this to be a fair submission for the reason that all counsels, including counsel representing the Petitioners in this matter addressed elaborate submissions on all the aforesaid three aspects. No doubt that, there was a prayer made for registration of F.I.R. and further investigation but then once we had examined the three aspects on merits we did not consider it appropriate to issue any directions, as prayed for by the Petitioners which automatically covered the direction for registration of FIR, prayed for.

7. Insofar as the aspect of pricing is concerned, the Court satisfied itself with the material made available. It is not the function of this Court to determine the prices nor for that matter can such aspects be dealt with on mere suspicion of persons who decide to approach the Court. The internal mechanism of such pricing would take care of the situation. On the perusal of documents we had found that one cannot compare apples and oranges. Thus, the pricing of the basic aircraft had to be compared which was

competitively marginally lower. As to what should be loaded on the aircraft or not and what further pricing should be added has to be left to the best judgment of the competent authorities.

8. It was the Petitioners' decision to have invoked the jurisdiction of this Court under Article 32 of the Constitution of India fully conscious of the limitation of the contours of the scrutiny and not to take recourse to other remedies as may be available. The Petitioners cannot be permitted to state that having so taken recourse to this remedy, they want an adjudication process which is really different from what is envisaged under the provisions invoked by them.

9. Insofar as the decision making process is concerned, on the basis of certain documents obtained, the Petitioners sought to contend that there was contradictory material. Present Court however, found that there were undoubtedly opinions expressed in the course of the decision making process, which may be different from the decision taken, but then any decision making process envisages debates and expert opinion and the final call is with the competent authority, which so exercised it. In this context, reference was made to (a) Acceptance of Necessity ('AON') granted by the Defence Acquisition Council ('DAC') not being available prior to the contract which would have determined the necessity and quantity of aircrafts; (b) absence of Sovereign Guarantee granted by France despite requirement of the Defence Procurement Procedure ('DPP'); (c) the oversight of objections of three expert members of the Indian Negotiating Team ('INT') regarding certain increase in the benchmark price; and (d) the induction of Reliance Aerostructure Limited ('RAL') as an offset partner.

10. It does appear that the endeavour of the Petitioners is to construe themselves as an appellate authority to determine each aspect of the contract and call upon the Court to do the same. Present Court do not believe this to be the jurisdiction to be exercised. All aspects were considered by the competent authority and the different views expressed considered and dealt with. It would well nigh become impossible for different opinions to be set out in the record if each opinion was to be construed as to be complied with before the contract was entered into. It would defeat the very purpose of debate in the decision making process.

11. There was no ground made out for initiating prosecution under Section 340 of CrPC.

12. The review petitions are without any merit and are accordingly dismissed, once again, re-emphasising that present Court's original decision

was based within the contours of Article 32 of the Constitution of India.

K.M. Joseph, J.

13. It must be noticed that the principle well-settled in regard to jurisdiction in review, is that a review is not an appeal in disguise. The applicant, in a review, is, on most occasions, told off the gates, by pointing out that his remedy lay in pursuing an appeal. In the case of a decision rendered by this Court, it is to be noticed that the underpinning based on availability of an appeal, is not available as this Court is the final Court and no appeal lies.

14. It is no doubt true that the Supreme Court Rules, 2013, certain powers are conferred on the Registrar as also on the Judge holding Court in Chambers and appeals, indeed, are provided in respect of certain orders passed by the Registrar.

15. The fact that no appeal lies from the judgment of this Court may not, however, result in the jurisdiction of this Court Under Article 137 of the Constitution being enlarged. However, when the Court is invited to exercise its power of review, this aspect may also be borne in mind, viz., that unlike the other courts from which an appeal may be provided either under the Constitution or other laws, or by special leave Under Article 136 of the Constitution, no appeal lies from the judgment of this Court, and it is in that sense, the final Court. The underlying assumption for the principle that a review is not an appeal in disguise, being that the decision is appealable, is really not available in regard to a decision rendered by this Court, is all that is being pointed out.

16. A review petition is maintainable if the impugned judgment discloses an error apparent on the face of the record. Unlike a proceeding in Certiorari jurisdiction, wherein the error must not only be apparent on the face of the record, it must be an error of law, which must be apparent on the face of the record, for granting review Under Article 137 of the Constitution read with Order XLVII Rule 1 of the Code of Civil Procedure, the error can be an error of fact or of law. No doubt, it must be apparent on the face of record. Such an error has been described as a palpable error or glaring omission. As to what constitutes an error apparent on the face of record, is a matter to be found in context of the facts of each case.

17. This is not a case where an old argument is being repeated in the sense that after it has been considered and rejected, it is re-echoed in review. It is an argument which was undoubtedly pressed in the original innings. It is not the fault of the party if the court chose not even to touch

upon it. No doubt, it may be different in a case where a ground or relief sought is ignored and it is found justified otherwise. But where a ground, which is based on principles laid down by a Constitution Bench of this Court, is not dealt with at all and it is complained of in review, it will rob the review jurisdiction of the very purpose it is intended to serve, if the complaint otherwise meritorious, is not heeded to.

18. It is one thing to say that with the limited judicial review, available to the Court, it did not find merit in the case of the Petitioners regarding failure to follow the DPP, presence of over-pricing, violation of Offset Guidelines to favour a party, and another thing to direct action on a complaint in terms of the law laid down by this Court. It is obvious that this Court was not satisfied with the material which was placed to justify a decision in favour of the Petitioners. It is also apparent that the Court has reminded itself of the fact that it was neither appropriate nor within the experience of the Court to step into the arena. It is equally indisputable that the entire findings are to be viewed from the standpoint of the nature of the jurisdiction it exercised. There are no such restrictions and limitations on an Officer investigating a case under the law. Present a case, making out the commission of cognizable offence, starting with the lodging of the FIR after, no doubt, making a preliminary inquiry where it is necessary, the fullest of amplitude of powers under the law, no doubt, are available to the Officer. The discovery of facts by Officer carrying out an investigation, is completely different from findings of facts given in judicial review by a Court. The entire proceedings are completely different.

19. In terms of Section 17A, no Police Officer is permitted to conduct any enquiry or inquiry or conduct investigation into any offence done by a public servant where the offence alleged is relatable to any recommendation made or decision taken by the public servant in discharge of his public functions without previous approval, inter alia, of the authority competent to remove the public servant from his Office at the time when the offence was alleged to have been committed. In respect of the public servant, who is involved in this case, it is Clause (c), which is applicable. Unless, therefore, there is previous approval, there could be neither inquiry or enquiry or investigation. It is in this context apposite to notice that the complaint, which has been filed by the Petitioners in Writ Petition (Criminal) No. 298 of 2018, moved before the first Respondent-CBI, is done after Section 17A was inserted. The complaint is dated 04.10.2018. Paragraph 5 sets out the relief which is sought in the complaint which is to register an FIR under

various provisions.

20. Therefore, Petitioners have filed the complaint fully knowing that Section 17A constituted a bar to any inquiry or enquiry or investigation unless there was previous approval. In fact, a request is made to at least take the first step of seeking permission under Section 17A of the 2018 Act. Writ Petition (Criminal) No. 298 of 2018 was filed on 24.10.2018 and the complaint is based on non-registration of the FIR. There is no challenge to Section 17A. Under the law, as it stood, both on the date of filing the petition and even as of today, Section 17A continues to be on the Statute Book and it constitutes a bar to any inquiry or enquiry or investigation. The Petitioners themselves, in the complaint, request to seek approval in terms of Section 17A but when it comes to the relief sought in the Writ Petition, there was no relief claimed in this behalf.

CHAPTER TEN

Girish Mittal Vs. Parvati V. Sundaram and Ors., 2019

Relevant Sections: Right To Information Act, 2005 - Section 8(1)(d); Right To Information Act, 2005 - Section 8(1)(e)

Hon'ble judges:L. Nageswara Rao and M.R. Shah, JJ.

No. of pdf pages in Original Judgment:5

Equivalent Citations:2019(4)ALLMR475, MANU/SC/0610/2019, 2019(6)SCALE804, 2019 (6) SCJ 334

Case note:

Contempt of Court - Disobedience of order - Withholding of information - Petitioner filed application seeking information from RBI regarding loss to nation in foreign derivative contract cases - No reply was given to certain query - Appellate Authority under RTI Act directed RBI to provide information for queries - Incomplete information was given for queries according to Petitioner - Central Information Commission directed RBI to furnish information in respect of queries - Reply was given by RBI but not satisfied with said information - RBI was intentionally withholding information in spite of directions issued by this Court that RBI was liable to provide information - Hence, present contempt petition - Whether there was any wilful and deliberate disobedience of directions issued by this Court in which RBI was directed to provide information regarding inspection reports and other documents to general public.

Facts:

The Petitioner filed an application seeking information from the RBI regarding the loss to the nation in the foreign derivative contract cases. The Petitioner also sought for a bank-wise breakup of the mark-to-market (MTM) losses. In all, the Petitioner sought information for certain queries in his application. The Appellate Authority under the RTI Act directed the RBI to provide information for queries. Incomplete information was given for queries 2, 9 and 10 according to the Petitioner. The Central Information Commission directed the RBI to furnish information in respect of queries. In obedience to the direction issued by the Central Information Commission, RBI furnished information for queries. However, the RBI filed a Writ Petition in the High Court aggrieved by the directions issued by the Central Information Commission qua query. After the judgment of this Court, RBI provided the information for query pertained to information regarding the market losses on account of currency derivatives. Not satisfied with the said information and being convinced that the RBI was intentionally withholding information in spite of the directions issued by this Court, Contempt Petition was filed by Petitioner.

Hon'ble Apex court held, while disposing off the petition:

(i) There was an element of public policy in punishing civil contempt, since administration of justice would be undermined if the order of any Court of law could be disregarded with impunity. There was no ambiguity in the judgment of this Court. After holding that there was no fiduciary relationship between the RBI and the other banks, this Court stressed the importance of the RTI Act, and held that it was in the interest of the general public that the information sought for by the Respondents therein had to be furnished. There was a specific reference to the inspection reports and the other materials, which were directed to be given to the Respondents therein. The only exception that was carved out by this Court was in the judgment, particularly, information which had a bearing on the security of the State etc. This court were not persuaded to accept the submission of contemnors that the judgment of this court requires reconsideration as this court could not consider the said submission while deciding the contempt petitions. The new disclosure policy was uploaded on the RBI website. The Petitioner was right in submitting that the new policy which replaces the disclosure policy directs various departments not to disclose information that was directed to be given by the judgment of this Court. The Respondents, had committed contempt of this Court by exempting disclosure of material that was directed to be given by this Court. In all fairness, contemnors had submitted that the disclosure policy shall be deleted from the website.

(ii) Though this court could have taken a serious view of the Respondents continuing to violate the directions issued by this Court, this court give them a last opportunity to withdraw the disclosure policy insofar as it contains exemptions which were contrary to the directions issued by this Court. The Respondents were duty bound to furnish all information relating to inspection reports and other material apart from the material that was exempted in the judgment. Any further violation shall be viewed seriously by this Court.

CHAPTER ELEVEN

K. Ananda Rao and Ors. Vs. S. S. Rawat and Ors., 2019

Relevant Sections: Constitution Of India - Article 142

Hon'ble judges: U.U. Lalit and M.R. Shah, JJ.

No. of pdf pages in Original Judgment: 16

Equivalent Citations: 2019(2)ALT305, 2019(1)ESC274(SC), MANU/SC/0336/2019, 2019(2)SCT236(SC), 2019(6)SLR204(SC), 2019(4)SCALE447, (2019)13SCC24, (2020)1SCC(LS)279, 2019 (10) SCJ 358

Case note:

Contempt of Court - Violation of directions - Present contempt petitions allege violation of judgment and order dated 9th August, 2017 passed by present Court - Whether mere expression "consequential benefits" would entitle concerned employees anything greater than what was contemplated in policy documents issued by State Government - Whether there had been any violation of directions issued by present Court on 9th August, 2017.

Facts:

Present Court while disposing of appeals after granting leave passed following order dated 9th August, 2017. Appellants approached present Court with certain grievances regarding their continuance in service upto 60 years of age. According to Government Companies/Corporation/Societies where they had been working and which were included in Schedules IX and X of Andhra Pradesh Reorganization Act of 2014, since Government had not granted approval to recommendation for continuance upto 60 years of age, they would not be entitled to continue until and unless Government takes a decision. When matters reached this Court, present Court in some cases had granted an interim order for continuance upto 60 years of age. State of Andhra Pradesh had brought to notice an order dated 8th August, 2017 issued by Government of Andhra Pradesh whereby such employees had been granted benefit of continuance upto 60 years of age. Government Order dated 8th August, 2017 permitting employees to continue upto age of 60 years had come into effect with effect from 2nd June, 2014. Therefore, all employees who had superannuated on account of attainment of age of 58 years on 2nd June, 2014 or thereafter were entitled to protection of their service upto 60 years of age and naturally to all consequential benefits arising therefrom. Contempt Petitions were filed by employees submitting that, in terms of order dated 9th August, 2017 all consequential benefits arising out of raising age of superannuation had to be extended to those who had superannuated on attaining age of 58 years on or after 2nd June, 2014. According to Petitioners the "consequential benefits" would and must include all back wages even for period the Petitioners had not actually worked in their respective organizations.

Hon'ble Apex court held, while dismissing the petition:

1. Initial orders were passed in matters pertaining to employees of Gurukulam or Society. All these orders were ex-parte orders. Insofar as employees of Society were concerned, it was submitted before this Court on 27th April, 2017 that a decision had already been taken by Society for raising age of superannuation and all that was required to be done in matter was only a formal expression in form of an appropriate legislation. Expression in order dated 5th May, 2017 that protection afforded would apply "to all similarly situated employees under Respondent institutions" was only in respect of employees of Society and not in relation to employees of all other entities mentioned in Schedules IX and X of 2014 Act. As a matter of fact, no notice was issued in any matter apart from matters pertaining to Society and all such other matters were simply tagged with main bunch of cases which came up before present Court and were disposed of on 9th August, 2017.

2. After policy decision was taken on 5th August, 2015 to raise age of superannuation from 58 years to 60 years in respect of employees of Society, that decision was kept in abeyance by Resolution dated 18th June, 2016. This Resolution stated that, Government had taken stock of all developments and had decided that issue regarding enhancement of age of superannuation in respect of employees of entities and institutions listed in IX and X Schedule of 2014 Act would be taken only after issue of division of assets and liabilities of concerned institutions between two States was settled and allotment of employees was finalized. This was followed by

GO dated 28th June, 2016. These developments were indicative that it was always in contemplation that if an employee had superannuated on attaining age of 58 years and was thereafter re-inducted in service with superannuation age being 60 years, he would not be entitled to any salary or normal emoluments for what was referred to as interregnum period or gap period, but would be entitled to certain notional benefits stipulated therein.

3. Even after disposal of petitions by High Court, matter was receiving attention of State Government which was evident from GO dated 8th August, 2017. It referred to background facts including requirement to have concerned Rules or Regulations regarding service conditions of employees in establishments in Schedule IX and X to be amended after due approval by Government and after consideration whether such establishments were finally capable and viable. One of factors which was recited was about that, issue of division of assets and liabilities was still pending and that allocation of employees was not yet finalized. GO modified earlier decision dated 27th June, 2017 to extent it had made such decisions prospective and now gave retrospective effect from 2nd June, 2014. It thus undoubtedly relaxed conditions as regards requirement to have Rules and Regulations amended after due approval by Government. It further stated that, if an employee was retired on attaining age of 58 years, he/she shall be reinstated and continued upto 60 years. However, this GO dated 8th August, 2017 did not in any way depart from or dilute principles as to what would be situation in case of interregnum period or gap period.

4. Purely on principle of parity, employees of institution or entities in Schedule IX and X of 2014 Act could not demand benefit of enhancement of age of superannuation from 58 years to 60 years. That benefit came to be conferred under policy documents and finally by GO dated 8th August, 2017. Thus, source was in those policy documents and naturally extent of benefits was also spelt out in those instruments issued by Government. Circular dated 28th June, 2016 which was more or less adopted in proceedings dated 11th June, 2018 must be taken to be governing criteria in respect of such employees. Unless and until that governing criteria was departed from specifically, mere expression "consequential benefits" would not entitle concerned employees anything greater than what was contemplated in policy documents issued by State Government.

5. There was no violation of orders passed by this Court. Every employee, who was similarly situated would be entitled to benefits conferred by policy documents referred to above but not for salary and

other emoluments for period they had not actually worked. Contempt petition dismissed.

CHAPTER TWELVE

Reliance Communication Limited and Ors. Vs. State Bank of India and Ors., 2019

Relevant Sections: Contempt Of Courts Act, 1971 - Section 12(4)
   Hon'ble judges: Rohinton Fali Nariman and Vineet Saran, JJ.
   No. of pdf pages in Original Judgment: 18
   Equivalent Citations:AIR2019SC1196, 2019(2)ALT60, 2019(4)ALD58, (2019)2CompLJ401(SC), [2019]151CLA11(SC), MANU/SC/0250/2019, 2019(3)SCALE428, 2019 (4) SCJ 416
   Case note:

Contempt of Court - Disobedience of order - Petitioner and Respondents entered into Managed Service Agreement whereby Petitioner agreed to provide Respondent managed services - Petitioner raised invoices from time to time in consideration of services provided, and on receiving no payment -Company Tribunal appointed Interim Resolution Professionals to carry out corporate insolvency resolution process - Appeals were filed against in Appellate Tribunal, who stayed orders and recorded statement of Respondent that amount would be paid within one hundred twenty days time - Respondent filed writ petition in this Court for closure of corporate insolvency resolution process - This Court recorded that timeline of one hundred twenty days shall be strictly adhered to - Respondent applied for extension of time for payment by sixty days, and this court made clear, as last opportunity, amount must be paid - Second application to extend time was moved, citing excuse of other spectrum not yet being saleable, which was dismissed as withdrawn - Hence, present petition - Whether there was any disobedience of order passed by this Court by Respondent companies.
   Facts:

Petitioner and Respondent companies entered into a Managed Service Agreement whereby Petitioner agreed to provide Respondent managed services, i.e., operation, maintenance, and management of network. Petitioner raised invoices from time to time in consideration of services provided, and on receiving no payment, ultimately issued three notices, under the Insolvency and Bankruptcy Code, 2016. Petitioner filed applications under Section 9 of the Code as operational creditors. The National Company Law Tribunal admitted the said petitions and appointed three Interim Resolution Professionals to carry out the corporate insolvency resolution process. Appeals were filed in Appellate Tribunal who, stayed the orders and recorded the statement that the matter had been agreed to be settled for a sum, which would be paid within one hundred twenty days' time. Respondent Companies filed a writ petition in this Court in which they asked for quashing/closure of the corporate insolvency resolution process in view of settlement of disputes between them and Petitioner. This Court recorded that the timeline of one hundred twenty days shall be strictly adhered to and payment was to be made. Respondent applied for extension of time for payment by sixty days, and this court made clear, as last opportunity, amount must be paid. The Second application to extend time was moved, citing excuse of other spectrum not yet being saleable. This Court made it clear that it was not inclined to grant any such extension, as a result of which, the second application for extension of time was dismissed as withdrawn.

Hon'ble Apex court held, whiledisposing off the petition:

(i) The undertakings given by the Chairmen of the Respondent companies were neither as per the Court's understanding of its order, nor the understanding of the three Companies themselves, as was clear from the undertakings given by the three Directors pursuant to the order. It was clear that the Respondent-Companies had no intention, at the very least, of adhering to the time limit of one hundred twenty days or to the extended time limit of sixty days plus, as was given by way of indulgence. The undertakings given on the footing that the amount would be paid only out of the sale of assets was false to the knowledge of the Petitioner Companies. This itself affects the administration of justice, and was therefore, contempt of court.

(ii) The contempt of this Court needs to be purged by payment of the sum together with interest till date. As stated by the letter, subject to any calculation error, an amount must be paid to Petitioner in addition to the deposit of amount made in the Registry of this Court. The Registry of this Court was directed to pay over the sum to Petitioner within a period of one week from today. The Respondent was directed to purge the contempt of this Court by payment to Petitioner within a period of four weeks from today. In default of such payment, the Chairmen who have given undertakings to this Court will suffer three months' imprisonment

CHAPTER THIRTEEN

Badri Vishal Pandey and Ors. Vs. Rajesh Mittal and Ors., 2019

Relevant Sections: Industrial Disputes Act, 1947 - Section 25-F; U.P. Industrial Disputes Act, 1947 - Section 6N, U.P. Industrial Disputes Act, 1947 - Section 6Q

Hon'ble judges: A.M. Khanwilkar and Hemant Gupta, JJ.

No. of pdf pages in Original Judgment: 7

Equivalent Citations: AIR2019SC289, 2019(2) ALJ 316, [2019(160)FLR645], MANU/SC/0010/2019, 2019(1)SCT550(SC), 2019(1)SCALE155, (2019)16SCC360, (2019)1UPLBEC1

Case note:

Contempt of Court - Termination - Disobedience of order - Petitioners were engaged as daily wager in U.P. Jal Nigam facing retrenchment of their services in pursuance to decision taken by Board - In pursuance to decision taken by Board Petitioner's services had been terminated - Writ petition was filed before High Court challenging order of termination which stand dismissed - Petitioner No. 1 raised industrial dispute which was referred to Labour Court - Labour Court ordered to pay compensation - Such Award was challenged by filing Writ Petition before High Court - In writ petition, order was of reinstatement but without back-wages - Jal Nigam filed Special Leave Petition against order of Single Bench - Such Special Leave Petitions were decided on basis of office order wherein it was resolved that in future, as and when any vacancy arises on daily wages/muster roll, preference would be given to terminated/retrenched employee of department - Hence, present contempt petition - Whether Respondents had violated any order passed by this Court.

Facts:

The Petitioners were engaged as daily wager in the U.P. Jal Nigam sometime in the year 1989 on various dates facing retrenchment of their services in pursuance to decision taken by the Board. U.P. Jal Nigam. Accordingly, in pursuance to decision taken by the Board Petitioner's services had been terminated. A Writ petition was filed before the High Court challenging order of termination which stand dismissed. The Petitioner No. 1 raised an industrial dispute which was referred to Labour Court. The Labour Court ordered to pay compensation. Such Award was challenged by the First Petitioner by filing Writ Petition. The order in the Writ Petition was of reinstatement but without back-wages. The Jal Nigam filed Special Leave Petition against the common order of the Single Bench. The Special Leave Petitions were decided on the basis of office order wherein it was resolved that in future, as and when any vacancy arises on daily wages/muster roll, the preference will be given to terminated/retrenched employee of the department.

Hon'ble Apex court held, while dismissing the appeal:

(i) The order had been passed on the basis of concession given on behalf of the workmen in light of the circular. There was no order of this Court to re-engage the workmen who were parties in the Special Leave Petitions. Therefore, in the absence of any specific and categorical direction of reinstatement, the Petitioners could not claim any right for reinstatement on the basis of the orders passed by this Court.

(ii) The Order of this Court was to take workmen on daily wage basis as per office order. The argument that they accepted the order under the impression that the workmen were being reinstated could not be accepted as the order had been passed on the basis of the circular which contemplates that the workmen shall be reinstated as per the seniority list as and when requirement in future arises. The Order of the Court could not be interpreted on the basis of the impressions which may be drawn by the Petitioners, in view of the specific order passed by this Court.

(iii) The argument that Group D posts were available against which Petitioners may be appointed was not tenable. The Group D posts were required to be filled on the basis of qualifications prescribed for filling up of such posts in the Rules as may be applicable to make appointments to such posts. The Petitioners, if eligible, could compete for such appointments. But merely they were once engaged on muster roll, they could not have right to seek regular appointment against Group D posts dehors the eligibility conditions prescribed in the Rules. The regular appointment can be made keeping in view the principles of public appointment which was by issuance of an advertisement giving opportunity to all eligible candidates to apply and to consider their suitability for the posts in non-discriminatory manner. The Petitioners appointed on muster roll basis could not claim regular appointment against the vacant Group D posts when the Award of the Labour Court was of reinstatement and not that of regular appointment.

(iv) Petitioners could not claim any grievance of not engaging them in pursuance of the order passed by this Court when this Court had disposed of the Special Leave Petitions in the light of circular which contemplates that the retrenched employees would be re-engaged in case any requirement arises and in order of seniority. Therefore, it could not be said that the Respondents had violated any order passed by this Court.

CHAPTER FOURTEEN

National Campaign Committee for Central Legislation on Construction Labour (NCC-CL) Vs. Union of India (UOI) and Ors., 2018

Relevant Sections: Building And Other Construction Workers (Regulation Of Employment And Conditions Of Service) Act, 1996 - Section 60; Constitution Of India - Article 21

Hon'ble judges: Madan B. Lokur and Deepak Gupta, JJ.

No. of pdf pages in Original Judgment: 28

Equivalent Citations: 2018(3)BomCR347, [2018(157)FLR489], 2018(4)KarLJ265, 2018(2)LLN1(SC), MANU/SC/0264/2018, 2018(1)SLJ354(SC), 2018(4)SCALE600, (2018)2SCC(LS)1, 2018 (6) SCJ 713 2018(2)ESC193(SC), (2018)IIILLJ13SC, 2018(2)SCT364(SC), (2018)5SCC607,

Case note:

Contempt of Court - Implementation of Provisions - Building and Other Construction Workers (Regulation of Employment and Conditions of Service) Act, 1996 (BOCW Act) - Building and Other Construction Workers' Welfare Cess Act, 1996 (Cess Act) - Present petition filed seeking implementation of BOCW Act and Cess Act in meaningful spirit - Whether construction workers denied benefits under BOCW Act and Cess Act

Facts:

The non-implementation of the BOCW Act violates the provisions which impose a primary responsibility on the State to ensure that all the needs of workers are met and that their basic rights are fully protected. The non-implementation also violates the right to live with dignity. It is averred that the BOCW Act and the Cess Act are based on an international convention. Hence, present petition filed seeking implementation of BOCW Act and Cess Act in meaningful spirit.

Hon'ble Apex court held, while disposing off the petitionl:

(i) The Statement of Objects and Reasons for the BOCW Act refers to 8.5 million construction workers (85 lakhs) in 1995-1996. They were the vulnerable Section of society who needed the support of the State for their safety, health and welfare. They have been consistently let down by the State and even directions given by this Court and by the Ministry of Labor and Employment has not brought about any substantive change. Governance is not about mouthing platitudes, or framing good looking schemes, but about action and it is quite clear to us that insofar as the rights of construction workers are concerned, that vulnerable Section of society has been badly let down by the governance structure. To make matters worse for them, the number of construction workers has increased 5-fold over the last 20 years, as estimated by the Ministry of Labor and Employment. The task before the State-to effectively implement the laws enacted by Parliament for the benefit and welfare of a vulnerable Section of society is enormous, and as the progression in the case shows, the State might well be unable to live up to the expectations of Parliament unless there is a strong will to bring about a positive change. State apathy in a situation such as this virtually amounts to exploitation of the construction workers, and if the State turns exploitative, there is little hope for vulnerable Sections of society.

(ii) The present Court directed the Ministry of Labor and Employment, the State Governments and the UTAs to put in place and strengthen the registration machinery, both for the registration of establishments as well as registration of construction workers. This should be done within a specified time-frame to be decided by them, but at the earliest. The Ministry, the State Governments and Union Territory Administration (UTA) in this regard has to establish and strengthen the machinery for the collection of cess. It is a matter of common knowledge that there is a tremendous amount of construction activity going on all over the country and there is no reason why establishments involved in the construction activity, both formal as well as non-formal, should not pay the cess, especially when they are utilizing the services of the construction workers. Similarly, there is no reason why the construction workers of these establishments should be denied their entitlements and benefits under the BOCW Act and other laws. As noted above, huge amounts are involved and the present Court would not be surprised if the quarterly collection of Rs. 5000 crores is perhaps the minimum-the cess collected could be much, much more, if the registration machinery and the collection machinery are strengthened and work to their potential.

(iii) The Ministry of Labor and Employment to frame one composite Model Scheme for the benefit of construction workers in consultation with all stakeholders including NGOs who are actually working at the grassroots level with construction workers. While there is urgency in framing such a Model Scheme, the present Court would caution the Ministry of Labor and Employment to make haste slowly and to prepare a Model Scheme that is comprehensive and can easily be implemented, is pragmatic and does not involve too much paperwork. The Ministry of Labor and Employment, the State Governments and the UTAs to conduct a social audit on the implementation of the BOCW Act so that in future there is better and more effective and meaningful implementation of the BOCW Act. If a mistake has occurred, and no doubt that hundreds of mistakes have occurred in the implementation of the BOCW Act, it is more appropriate to admit the mistake for a better future rather than to justify it or continue to repeat the mistake. This is more so in the case of the BOCW Act where crores of men, women and children are involved on a day-to-day basis and Parliament has thought it appropriate to legislate for their benefit. The sanctity of laws enacted by Parliament must be acknowledged-laws are enacted for being adhered to and not for being flouted. The Rule of law must be respected and along with it the human rights and dignity of building and construction workers must also be respected and acknowledged, to avoid a complete breakdown of the BOCW Act compounded by serious violations of Part III of the Constitution guaranteeing fundamental rights.

CHAPTER FIFTEEN

Anil Kalra Vs. J. D. Pandey and Ors., 2015

Case Category:
CONTEMPT OF COURT MATTERS - CIVIL CONTEMPT MATTERS
Hon'ble judges: Dipak Misra and Prafulla C. Pant, JJ.
No. of pdf pages in Original Judgment: 5
Equivalent Citations: 2016(1) ALJ 688, 2015 (113) ALR 397, 2015 (6) AWC 6005 (SC), 2015X AD (S.C.) 457, MANU/SC/1085/2015, 2015(2)RCR(Rent)417, 2015(10)SCALE241, 2015 (10) SCJ 778

Case note:
Tenancy - Execution of Form-D - Application for release of building - Competent Authority called for report - Report of Rent Control Inspector submitted - Vacancy declared - Order for release of building - Favour of Appellant and co-landlords - Form-D issued - Review petition by unauthorised occupants - Dismissed by Competent Authority - Rent revision filed - Decided in favour of Respondents - Writ Petition - Challenged order of Revisional Court - Allowed with direction - Delivery of possession be re-initiated - Respondents filed application for recall - Dismissed - Litigation attained finality - Special Leave Petition dismissed - Appellant applied - Execution of Form-D - Rent Control Officer directed eviction - Respondents offered - Possession of thirteen rooms only - Eviction proceedings stalled - Contempt petition filed - Single judge ordered compliance - Contempt Appeal by Respondents - Dismissed as not maintainable - Respondents filed Special Appeal (Intra Court Appeal) - High Court rejected preliminary objection of Appellants - Appeal through Special leave - Whether the Civil Appeal preferred by the landlord deserves to be allowed

Facts:

The property in dispute is covered under Uttar Pradesh Urban Buildings (Regulation of Letting, Rent and Eviction) Act, 1972 (UP Act 13 of 1972) and was settled in favour of Rai Bahadur Lakshman Das, but physical possession could not be delivered as the building was in occupation of several tenants. Appellant Anil Kalra, along with his brother, sister and two others, became landlords through heirs of Rai Bahadur Lakshman Das by way of sale deeds. An application was moved Under Section 16(1)(b) of UP Act 13 of 1972 for release of the building for demolition and reconstruction before the Competent Authority.

Competent Authority called for a report from Rent Control Inspector, who inspected and reported that the Office of Cane Commissioner (tenant on part of the building) was in the midst of vacating the same and that Respondent No. 2 and Respondent No. 3 (both sons of Dr. J.D. Pandey), under the banner of M/s. Swargiya Sanjay Gandhi Sahkari Avas Samiti Ltd., had unauthorizedly occupied the building. On perusal of the report of the Rent Control Inspector and after inviting objections of concerned parties, vacancy was declared. The Competent Authority issued the order for release of the building in favour of the Appellant and co-landlords. When after issuance of Form-C unauthorized occupants failed to vacate the building, Form-D was issued.

The unauthorized occupants filed a review petition before the Competent Authority, but the same was dismissed with the finding that the occupants were transferees from a samiti, which has no title or authority to occupy the building. On this a Rent Revision was filed by Respondent Nos. 1 to 3 which was decided in favour of said Respondents. The Appellant and co-landlords filed the Writ Petition before the High Court challenging the order passed by the revisional court which was allowed by the High Court, with the direction that the proceedings for delivery of possession to the landlord shall be re-initiated from the stage they were stayed. The application for recall, filed by Respondent Nos. 1 to 3, was dismissed. That round of litigation attained finality with the dismissal of Special Leave Petition on 10.12.2002, by this Court.

The Appellant, thereafter, moved application for execution of Form-D before the Rent Control Officer and said authority issued direction for execution. Respondent Nos. 1 to 3 offered to give possession of thirteen rooms only, and got the eviction proceedings stalled against unauthorized occupants. The Appellant filed Contempt Petition before the High Court in which Respondent Nos. 1 to 3 expressed willingness to hand over possession of thirteen rooms only and not the building. The single Judge, hearing the contempt petition, directed Rent Control Officer to comply the order passed in the writ petition, against which Special Leave Petition had been dismissed. Respondent Nos. 1 to 3 filed Contempt Appeal against the interim order passed by the Judge hearing the contempt petition which was dismissed as not maintainable. Thereafter, the Respondents filed Special Appeal (Intra Court Appeal) before the High Court. The High Court rejected the preliminary objection that no Special Appeal is maintainable against the order of the Judge hearing the contempt petition. Hence, this appeal through special leave, before us. Connected Civil Appeal Nos. 5688-89 of 2007 are filed by Respondent Nos. 1 to 3 of the Civil Appeal No. 3763 of 2007 against the judgment and orders dated 1.12.2006 and 8.12.2006, passed by the High Court in Criminal Miscellaneous Case No. 265 of 2006 and Contempt Appeal No. 51 of 2006.

Hon'ble Apex court held:

(I) The Respondents failed to show that under what authority the building was being occupied by Respondent Nos. 1 to 3 and let out to various occupants in violation of Section 11 of the UP Act 13 of 1972. There is no allotment order issued in favour of any of the alleged occupants Under Section 16 of the UP Act 13 of 1972. It is not in dispute that the building is old... in any case the building was covered under the Act and not exempted under any of the clauses mentioned in Section 2 of the UP Act No. 13 of 1972.[6] and[7]

(II) In view of law laid down by this Court, and considering the facts and circumstances of the present case, and conduct of Respondents whereby persons in large number inducted unauthorisedly by them without any allotment order, Civil Appeal No. 3763 of 2007, filed by the landlord, deserves to be allowed, and Civil Appeal Nos. 5688-89 of 2007, filed by the Respondents are liable to be dismissed. We order accordingly. We further direct the Competent Authority to execute the Form-D. However, keeping in mind that there are several occupants (inducted unauthorisedly without any allotment order), on humanitarian ground they are allowed three months' time from today to vacate the premises voluntarily, whereafter they or anyone occupying in their place along with Respondent Nos. 1 to 3 in Civil Appeal No. 3763 of 2007, shall be forcibly dispossessed within 48 hours in compliance of this order, as directed above.[14]

(III) The District Magistrate and the Senior Superintendent of Police, Lucknow, are directed to provide every assistance in execution of the order of release, affirmed by the High Court in Writ Petition (R/C) No. 183 of 1991 on 26.5.1999. We also clarify that the landlords are not allowed to let out the released building (in the existing condition), and they shall demolish the building for reconstruction for which the building has been released by the authority concerned.[14]

CHAPTER SIXTEEN

In Re: Mohit Chaudhary, 2017

Relevant Sections: SUPREME COURT RULES, 2013 - Order IV Rule 10

Hon'ble judges:J.S. Khehar, Dr. D.Y. Chandrachud and Sanjay Kishan Kaul, JJ.

No. of pdf pages in Original Judgment: 12

Equivalent Citations:2017(178)AIC118, AIR2017SC3836, 2017(4)Crimes439(SC), (2017)6MLJ502, MANU/SC/1009/2017, 2017(3)RCR(Criminal)936, 2017(9)SCALE65, (2017)16SCC78, 2017 (7) SCJ 713, 2017 (3) WLN 154 (SC)

Case note:

Contempt of Court - Allegation against Registry - Rule 10 of Order IV of Supreme Court Rules, 2013 - Allegations sought to be made against Registry with insinuations directed even against Judges - Advocate-on-Record had committed contempt in face of Court, by making such insinuations and allegations, and thus notice of contempt was issued to Contemnor - Hence, present suo motu contempt petition - Whether some consequences must follow on Contemnor for his conduct.

Facts:

Contemnor sought to contend that a great manipulation had occurred in the Registry of present Court in order to favour the opposite party with the objective of Bench Hunt. The contemnor was an Advocate-on-Record. The listing had been based on a judicial direction and had not been determined at the hands of the Registry of the Court. The allegations sought to be made against the Registry with insinuations directed even against the Judges, led to prima facie satisfaction, that the Advocate-on-Record had committed contempt in the face of the Court, by making such insinuations and allegations, and thus notice of contempt was issued to Contemnor. Hence, present suo motu contempt petition.

Hon'ble Apex court held, while disposing off the petition:

(i) It was not an innocent act, an innocuous endeavor but a well thought out decision to tread an unfortunate path which the existing Advocate-on-Record was unwilling to do. The objective was only to assist the client by somehow seeking shifting of the Bench. The allegations made against the Registry were false and there were innuendoes against the Court. The endeavor failed. Every action had to have an outcome. The Contemnor thus must face some consequences of his conduct. The privilege of being an Advocate-on-Record under the Rules had clearly been abused by the Contemnor. The conduct was not becoming of an advocate much less an advocate-on-record in the Supreme Court.

(ii) Rule 10 of Order IV of Rules makes it clear, whether on the complaint of any person or otherwise, in case of misconduct or a conduct unbecoming of an Advocate-on-Record, the Court may make an order removing his name from the register of Advocate-on-Record permanently, or for a specified period. The present case was clearly one where present Court was of the opinion that the conduct of the Contemnor was unbecoming of an Advocate-on-Record. The pre-requisites of the proviso were met, by the reason of the Bench being constituted itself by the Chief Justice, and the Contemnor being aware of the far more serious consequences, which could have flowed to him. The Contemnor was not permitted to practice as an Advocate-on-Record, for a period of one month.

CHAPTER SEVENTEEN

Rajiv Dawar Vs. High Court of Delhi, 2017

Relevant Sections: Contempt Of Courts Act, 1971 - Section 2(C); Contempt Of Courts Act, 1971 - Section 10; Contempt Of Courts Act, 1971 - Section 15; Constitution Of India - Article 215

Hon'ble judges: Kurian Joseph and R. Banumathi, JJ.

No. of pdf pages in Original Judgment: 2

Equivalent Citations:2017(178)AIC141, 2017ALLMR(Cri)3542, 2017(165)DRJ312, MANU/SC/0969/2017, 2018(1)RCR(Criminal)335, 2017(8)SCALE385, (2018)12SCC437

Case note:

Contempt of Court - Conviction - Maintainability thereof - Section 2(c), 10 and 15 of Contempt of Courts Act, 1971 and Article 215 of Constitution of India - Present appeal filed against order whereby Appellant was convicted under Section 2(c) read with Section 10 and 15 of Act and under Article 215 of Constitution - Whether conviction order passed by High Court was maintainable.

Facts:

Present appeal filed against order whereby the Appellant was convicted under Section 2(c) read with Section 10 and 15 of Contempt of Courts Act and under Article 215 of the Constitution of India.

Hon'ble Apex court held, while allowing the appeal:

(i) The Disciplinary Authority having completely absolved the Appellant and the procedural safeguards having not been followed and also that the Appellant had complied with the direction to refund the money, the conviction and sentence imposed on the Appellant was set aside.

CHAPTER EIGHTEEN

Satwant Singh Vs. Malkeet Singh, 2017

Relevant Sections: CODE OF CRIMINAL PROCEDURE, 1973 (CrPC) - Section 438; INDIAN PENAL CODE, 1860 (IPC) - Section 307

Hon'ble judges: Kurian Joseph and R. Banumathi, JJ.

No. of pdf pages in Original Judgment: 2

Equivalent Citations: 2017(178)AIC116, AIR2017SC3607, 2017(4)AJR420, 2017(6)ALD119, MANU/SC/0952/2017, (2018)11SCC616

Case note:

Contempt of Court - Addition of charge - Conviction - Sections 438 of Code of Criminal Procedure, 1973 and Section 307 of Indian Penal Code, 1860 - Both Single Judge and the Division Bench had taken view that once Respondent/Appellant had been granted interim bail under Section 438 of Code of Criminal Procedure as per order, his arrest on charge which had been later on added under Section 307, Indian Penal Code constitutes contempt - Appellant was punished for civil contempt - Hence, present appeal - Whether there was wilful or deliberate attempt to violate Court order.

Facts:

Both Single Judge and the Division Bench had taken the view that once the Respondent had been granted interim bail under Section 438 of Code of Criminal Procedure as per order, his arrest on a charge which had been later on added under Section 307, Indian Penal Code constitutes contempt. Hence, present appeal.

Hon'ble Apex court held, while allowing the appeal:

(i) This addition of charge was based on a subsequent investigation on the direction issued by the Senior Superintendent of Police after disposal of the Section 438 petition by the High Court and the arrest also was carried out on his instruction. It was significant to note that when the First Information Report was originally registered Section 307 had been included. It was deleted based on the instruction of a superior officer. After such deletion only, the Respondent approached the High Court. The Appellant had tendered an apology explaining his conduct before present Court in the civil appeal. The Appellant had tendered unconditional apology explaining that he only carried out the instruction of the Superintendent and he bona fide understood the order passed by the Court to mean that the Respondent was entitled to protection under Section 438, Code of Criminal Procedure only in respect of those offences reflected in the order. Section 307, Indian Penal Code having been added subsequently there was no impediment in proceeding with the investigation after arresting the Respondent on that count. It was a plausible explanation to show that there was no wilful or deliberate attempt to violate the Court order. No doubt, it would have been certainly more appropriate to apprise the Court on this development and seek modification. There was no intentional move to overstep the order of the Court.

CHAPTER NINETEEN

Jaghbir Singh and Ors. Vs. P. K. Tripathi and Ors., 2017

Relevant Sections: DELHI MUNICIPAL CORPORATION ACT, 1957 - Section 345A

Hon'ble judges: J.S. Khehar, C.J.I. and Dr. D.Y. Chandrachud, J.

No. of pdf pages in Original Judgment: 10

Equivalent Citations: MANU/SC/0882/2017, 2017(8)SCALE181, (2017)16SCC372, 2017 (10) SCJ 665

Case note:

Contempt of Court - Sealing of premises - Maintainability thereof - Court directed all industrial units in non-confirming/residential areas of State to be closed down/shifted - Notice was issued to Petitioner/ Contemnor for closing down industrial unit in residential premises - Sub-Divisional Magistrate issued sealing memo to seal premises of Contemnor - Hence, present petition by Contemnor - Whether contempt petition was maintainable.

Facts:

The Court had directed all industrial units in non-confirming/residential areas of State to be closed down/shifted. The notice records that the above directive came to be published through public notices, as well as, in leading newspapers. The notice showed that the Contemnor was still using the premises for running a mill in the residential area. Alternative industrial premises had been allotted to the Contemnor and in consonance with the terms and conditions of the fresh allotment letter, he was required to close down the industrial unit in the residential premises, yet he had not done so. Consequent upon the issuance of the notice, the Sub-Divisional Magistrate, issued a sealing memo by which the same premises were again ordered to be sealed. The Contemnor moved a representation requesting the Sub-

Divisional Magistrate, to de-seal the premises. Contemnor was unsuccessful in obtaining any favourable order from the Sub-Divisional Magistrate. Hence, present petition by Contemnor.

Hon'ble Apex court held, while disposing off the petition:

(i) The Contemnor consciously and deliberately disobeyed the directions issued by the Court from the documents available on the record of the case. The personal affidavit filed by the Contemnor proved that the Contemnor was personally aware of the directions of the Court. The Contemnor continued to violate the directions, and overlook the undertaking given to the Court till he was again caught committing the breach by the Sub-Divisional Magistrate. The Contemnor by his acts of omission and commission, had committed contempt. The Contemnor had made a grave mistake and requested that he be pardoned. He also tendered an unqualified apology to the Court. The parameters should be laid down for violation of the two orders passed by the present Court.

CHAPTER TWENTY

Vitusah Oberoi and Ors. Vs. Court of its own motion, 2017

Relevant Sections: CONSTITUTION OF INDIA - Article 215; CONSTITUTION OF INDIA - Article 219
 Hon'ble judges:T.S. Thakur, C.J.I. and A.M. Khanwilkar, J.
 No. of pdf pages in Original Judgment: 7
 Equivalent Citations:2017(170)AIC43, AIR2017SC225, 2017ALLMR(Cri)454, 2017(1)ACR462, 2017 (120) ALR 708, 2017 (2) ALT (Crl.)8 (A.P.), 2017(2)BomCR(Cri)12, 2017(1)CLJ(SC)129, 2017(1)CGLJ337, 2017(3)Crimes43(SC), 2017CriLJ961, I(2017)CCR65(SC), 2017(1)J.L.J.R.322, 2017-1-LW(Crl)317, MANU/SC/0004/2017, 2017(1)N.C.C.288, 2017(1)PLJR440, 2017(1)RCR(Civil)874, 2017(1)RCR(Criminal)983, 2017(1)SCALE83, (2017)2SCC314, 2017 (1) SCJ 416, 2017(1)UC225
 Case note:
Contempt of Court - Suo motu proceedings - Publication of article - Division Bench of High Court found Appellants guilty of contempt and directed to remain present in person before High Court for being heard on quantum of sentence to be awarded to them - Hence, present appeal - Whether suo motu proceedings initiated by High Court on account of the publication of the articles, stories and write ups questioning the propriety of certain orders passed by Justice, were sustainable
 Facts:
Appellants No. 1 and 2 were Editor and City Editor respectively of Mid Day, an English Daily Newspaper. Appellant No. 3 happened to be the Printer and Publisher of the papers while Appellant No. 4 was a Cartoonist

working for the said paper. The genesis of the suo motu contempt proceedings initiated by the High Court lay in a story that appeared in 'Mid Day' under the title "Injustice". The substance of the publication brought to light the alleged misuse of the official residence of Justice who demitted office as Chief Justice of India, by the same being shown as the registered office of three companies promoted by Justice's sons. A second story pointed out that Justice's son had entered into a partnership with shopping malls and commercial complex developers just before Justice passed orders for sealing of commercial establishments running in residential areas. This, according to the story, benefited the partnership business of Justice's sons. The third story that quoted some senior lawyer's saying that if the facts about Justice's sons' partnership business benefitting from the orders of Justice's Bench were true, then Justice should not have heard the case. The paper also carried in the same issue a cartoon by Appellant No. 4 showing as if Justice 's family had benefited from the orders passed by Justice's Bench. An advocate appeared to have placed a copy of the newspaper before a Division Bench of the High Court to draw the attention of the Court about the Article published in the said paper maligning the former Chief Justice of India and tending to lower the image of the judiciary in the eyes of the common man. The High Court initiated suo-motu contempt proceedings and issued show cause notices to Appellants. The explanation offered by the Appellants notwithstanding the High Court found the Appellants guilty of contempt and directed them to remain present in person for being heard on the question of quantum of sentence that may be awarded to them. The present appeal assailed the correctness of the said order.

Videos & Tv Shows On Law & Exim

List of some important videos & TV shows on Law & EXIM by Adv. Jayprakash Somani on his YouTube Channel 'Jayprakash Somani EXIM & Legal'

Legal Videos: Hindi -English

1) SLP in Supreme Court / Special Leave Petitions in the Supreme Court of India
2) Transfer of Civil & Criminal Cases by the Supreme Court of India / Transfer of Matrimonial Cases
3) Appellate Jurisdiction of the Supreme Court of India
4) Jurisdictions of the Supreme Court of India
5) Public Interest Litigation in the Supreme Court of India / PIL in Supreme Court
6) Article 32 Writ Petitions in the Supreme Court of India
7) Bail Matters Top 10 Supreme Court Cases
8) FIR Quashing in High Court & Supreme Court
9) Bail & Anticipatory Bail Matters in Supreme Court
10) Insolvency & Bankruptcy Matters in the Supreme Court
11) Insolvency & Bankruptcy Code 2016 Part 1
12) Insolvency & Bankruptcy Code 2016 Part 2
13) Insolvency & Bankruptcy Code 2016 Part 3
14) Corporate Liquidation Process
15) Supreme Court Rules & Procedures Webinar of 2.5 hour on Zoom
16) RDDBFI Act, 1993 (Introduction)
17) The Indian Contact Act 1872
18) Negotiable Instruments Act (Introduction)
19) How to avoid matrimonial disputes & some more videos
20) SEBI Matters in the Supreme Court
21) Matrimonial Matters: Supreme Court's 20 Case Laws
22) Consumer Matters Supreme Court's 20 Case Laws
23) Service Matters Supreme Court's 20 Case Laws
24) How to Search Lawyer for Your Matter
25) Property Matters Supreme Court's 20 Case Laws
26) Bail Matters: Supreme Court's 20 Case Laws
27) Supreme Court / High Court Vacation Benches

28) 69000 Teacher's Recruitment Matters of UP Government in the Supreme Court
29) Contempt of Court Matters in the Supreme Court
30) Advocate Act's Matters in the Supreme Court
31) Business Law Matters in the Supreme Court
32) Banking Matters in the Supreme Court
33) Labour Law Matters in the Supreme Court
34) Arbitration Matters in the Supreme Court
35) Careers in Law -Zoom Webinar by Adv. Jayprakash Somani
36) Civil Matters in the Supreme Court
37) Consumer Protection Act | Consumer Matters in the Supreme Court
38) Corporate Matters in the Supreme Court
39) Criminal Matters in the Supreme Court
40) Role of Respondent in the Supreme Court of India
41) Motor Vehicle Accident Matters in Supreme Court with case laws
42) Article 131 Original Suits in Supreme Court
43) PIL in Supreme Court/ Public Interest Litigations in the Supreme Court of India'
44) CAB Citizenship Amendment Bill is not Unconstitutional
45) Supreme Court of India Cases & Process – Marathi
46) Legal Services Export / Export of Legal Services
47) Transfer of Matrimonial Cases by the Supreme Court of India
48) Public Interest Litigation PIL
49) The Specific Relief Act (Introduction)
50) Corporate Insolvency Resolution Process CIRP
51) ABMM's Career 5 - Careers in Law
52) Transfer of cases by Supreme Court
53) Writ Petitions in High Court & Supreme Court of India
54) Supreme Court Jurisdictions - Appeals, SLP, Writ Petitions, Transfer, Original, Review, Curative
55) LEGAL INDIA TV Show: Cases Handled in Supreme Court
56) Corporate Liquidation Process
57) Legal Services Export / Export of Legal Services

EXIM Videos: Hindi -English
1) Yes, I can do Import Export Business Easily! 36 points excellent video in Hindi
2) Yes, I can do Import Export Business Easily! 36 points excellent video in English

VIDEOS & TV SHOWS ON LAW & EXIM

3) Import Export Business – Hindi video
4) Import Export Business - English video
5) Export Import Marathi TV Interview
6) Scope for Commerce Students in International Business- TV Show
7) Scope for Management Student in International Business- TV Show
8) Scope for Engineering Students in International Business – TV Show
9) Women in International Business- TV Show
10) How to do Import Export Business Successfully!'
11) Where one can get full information on Import Export Business?
12) What to do import & export?
13) Import Export Workshop/ Training/Course/ Diploma
14) How to Start Import Export Business & How to grow it. Live Webinar
15) Success Stories & Failure Stories in Import & Export Business
16) For MSME Scope in Export & Import...
17) Exports In Agri. & Food Products – English & some more videos
18) Exports to Dubai, Aabudhabii. e. UAE
19) Jewellery Exports from India
20) How to attend EXIM workshop to become excellent Exporter
21) Import Export Best Training Course – Online & Offline
22) Agri Product Export
23) Scope for Woman in International Business
24) Management Graduates Scope in International Business
25) Pharma Product's Export
26) Best Import Export Course | Practical Training | Aaronica Global Exim
27) Import Export Business for Commerce Graduates
28) How Do I Get Export Orders? Finding International Buyers
29) What Is APEDA In Import Export Business?
30) Which Is The Best Product To Export From India?
31) EXIM Remark by Manoj Kumar Faridabad
32) EXIM Remarks by Mahesh Telangana
33) What Licenses I Need To Start Import/ Export?
34) How Can I Increase My Import Export Business?
35) Which Is Best B2B Website For Import/Export Business?
36) Export Import Management with Global Marketing
37) How to Start Export Import Business | 51 Points Video
38) Scope for Commerce & Other Graduates in International Business

VIDEOS & TV SHOWS ON LAW & EXIM

39) BE A SUCCESSFUL EXPORTER FOR OUR NATION - Marathi video
40) Export of Textile, Cotton, Agri., Food, & other products & services
41) Exports from MP, CG, MH, GJ & CA in Fresh Fruits & Vegetables
42) Exports in Agri. & Food Products- Hindi
43) Start your Online/E-Commerce Business
44) How to Start Export Import Business & Grow it
45) Exports in Textile & Other Products
46) Start and grow EXIM business - Live English Webinar
47) 'Import Export Business!' Why, Who, What & How can one do it easily!!
48) Live: Export of Product & Services During & After Lock Down Period
49) Frauds in Import Export Business
50) Import Export for Business Man
51) Import & Export for Women
51) Import & Export for Graduate & Post - Graduate Students
52) Agriculture Exports from India
53) Digital Marketing Setup - Marathi
54) 2nd Secret of Successful Businessman
55) Digital Marketing Set up
56) Legal Services Export / Export of Legal Services
57) Export & Import with UAE
58) Service Exports / Exports by Service Providers
59) Import Export Workshop/ Training/Course/ Diploma
60) Exports & Imports with USA
61) Selection on Product for Export
62) Top Products Exported from India
63) What to do import & export?
64) ABMM Career 2 - 'Careers in Business & Industries
65) How to do Import Export Business Successfully!'
66) 5 Secrets of Successful Businessman
67) Export from MP, Chhattisgarh & Vidarbha Nagpur
68) EXIM Hindi - Textile & Apparel Export
69) EXIM Hindi - Export Import Practical Training In Delhi, Kolkata, Mumbai and Pune
70) Import Export Business
71) Import Export Business Hindi
72) Import Export Business English video

73) Import Export Business Marathi

74) Women in International Business by Exim Guru Adv. Jayprakash Somani

75) Opportunities in Foreign Trade- Adv. Jayprakash Somani's special interview

List Of Books

List of Adv. Jayprakash Somani's Books
1. Supreme Court of India's Leading Case Laws on 'Insolvency & Bankruptcy Code 2016'
2. Bail Matters – Supreme Court's Latest Leading Case Laws
3. Arbitration Matters- Supreme Court's Latest Leading Case Laws
4. Property Matters - Supreme Court's Latest Leading Case Laws
5. Matrimonial Matters- Supreme Court's Latest Leading Case Laws
6. Election Matters- Supreme Court's Latest Leading Case Laws
7. SEBI Matters- Supreme Court's Latest Leading Case Laws
8. Banking Matters- Supreme Court's Latest Leading Case Laws
9. Service Matters- Supreme Court's Latest Leading Case Laws
10. Contempt of Court Matters- Supreme Court's Latest Leading Case Laws
11. Consumer Protection Matters- Supreme Court's Latest Leading Case Laws
12. Corporate Law- Supreme Court's Latest Leading Case Laws
13. Mental Cruelty Against Husband - Supreme Court's Latest Leading Case Laws
14. Armed Force Tribunal - Supreme Court's Latest Leading Case Laws
15. Acquittal From 376 - Supreme Court's Latest Leading Case Laws

These Books are available online at

1. **Notion Press:**https://notionpress.com/author/jayprakash_somani
2. **Amazon:**https://www.amazon.in/s?k=jayprakash+somani
3. **Flipkart:**https://www.flipkart.com/search?q=Jayprakash%20Somani

www.ingramcontent.com/pod-product-compliance
Lightning Source LLC
Chambersburg PA
CBHW070815220526
45466CB00002B/669